MEMORIES OF A
RHONDDA BOY

MEMORIES OF A RHONDDA BOY

(A short auto-biography of my formative years)

by

Bryan W. Sheldon

MEMORIES OF A RHONDDA BOY

©   B.W. SHELDON (2017)

Contents

INTRODUCTION

In the middle of the 20th century, if you mentioned the Rhondda Valley, it would conjure up pictures of coal mines, surrounded by rows and rows of drab terraced cottages, nestling among bare hills topped with coal tips. Today, the pits are gone, many cottages are brightly coloured, and the hills are green and wooded. But the memories remain!

My name is Bryan William Sheldon. Normally called 'Bry', when I was in school I also answered to, 'Bryan with a 'Y'". It separated me from the other 'Brians' in my class, who spelt their name with an 'I'. Born just before the second world war and brought up in the Rhondda during a period of austerity and rationing, I was the only child in a household of adults. I spent many hours alone but was never lonely. Solitude suits some and I was fortunate that it suited me, because circumstances often demanded it.

I had a second quality that was also of benefit – I was never envious of others who had more than I had or who seemed to have an easier life than mine. I took life as it came – it was what it was – and I rolled with the punches!

CHAPTER ONE

A SHORT HISTORY LESSON

The Rhondda valleys, Rhondda Fawr and Rhondda Fach, (hereafter called the Rhondda), were, between 1860 and 1939, one of the world's most important coal mining regions. With a combined length of only 20 miles it was home to over 70 collieries and drift mines. Every village had its colliery which drew in workers from other parts of Wales, and across the border in England. The population of the valley peaked in the mid 1920's at about 165,000. At that time there were over 4000 working the Cambrian pit in Clydach Vale, 3000 working the Lewis Merthyr Colliery and 2000 the Parc.

The industrial history of the valley in the early 1900's was especially turbulent. It was a never-ending narrative of mining disasters, disputes and conflict, punctuated by 'the Great War' of 1914/18. If it were to be captured on canvas, the artist would need a full pallet of greys and blacks.

COLLIERY DISASTERS

The price of coal has always included the loss of life. In the Rhondda in 1905 two disasters occurred within four months of each other. 31

7

lives were lost at the Cambrian Colliery, Clydach Vale, and a further 119 were lost at the National Colliery, Wattstown. Although not in the Rhondda, the Senghenydd pit disaster of 1913, which saw the death of 439 men and boys, further added to the atmosphere of unease that pervaded the coalfield. Most disasters, including the afore-mentioned three, were the result of explosions – the ignition of 'firedamp', a highly explosive gas consisting of methane and hydrogen, which was present in many of the coal seams.

There were occasions when the colliery siren would sound over the valley, indicating that there had been a 'fall' or an explosion underground. Families would gather at the pithead, hoping for good news but anticipating bad. The women of every village were called upon to bury those of their men who lost their lives. In addition, there were the countless numbers who suffered injury underground and were compelled to find some other way to eke out a living. It was the not-unreasonable understanding of the workers then, that the safety of the miners was sacrificed in the pursuit of profit for the coal-owners.

THE TONYPANDY RIOTS

While the relationship between colliery workers and coal owners was always strained, 1910 and

1926 are marked out as particular identifiable flashpoints.

The 1910 flashpoint concerned a conflict between Rhondda mine owners and workers. It had escalated to a point where, in November of that year, violence erupted at a demonstration in Tonypandy. The dispute came to a climax because some 950 miners from the Ely pit in Penygraig had been locked out. This action caused anger in the workers, which overflowed into violence. Shops were looted and property belonging to the colliery owners was damaged or destroyed. Casualties were suffered by both sides, by members of the constabulary, who sought to quell the disturbance, and by the demonstrators. An appeal by the Glamorgan Chief Constable to the War Office resulted in military re-enforcements. It was decided to send a detachment of Lancashire Fusiliers, although initially they were held in reserve away from the troubles. When they finally arrived, they were used to maintain order and stop picketing. Although things calmed down after the rioting of 7th and 8th of November, skirmishes and unease remained in the area until the August of 1911, when the miners were forced to accept the original offer of 2s 3d per ton, and return to work.

The events of November 1910 are collectively known as 'the Tonypandy riots' which have passed into valley folk-lore. That a dispute existed between the coal-owners who were members of the Cambrian Combine (a cartel created to fix coal prices and wages), and the miners, is certain, but many of the facts seem to have been embellished. However, it is the perception of the actions of authorities (the police, the war office and the home office), that has coloured the opinions of the population of the valley and endured. As a result, the voting habits of the Rhondda public have been polarised, and the valley is now one of the most secure seats for the Labour party. As far as Rhondda residents were concerned, the reputation of Winston Churchill, who was then Home Secretary, was tarnished beyond redemption.

THE 1914/18 GREAT WAR

Added to the loss of those who died underground was the loss of those who died in the 1914/18 conflict. Many Rhondda men volunteered for military service, while others were 'called up' when conscription was introduced in 1916. My grandfather, who had worked at the coal face, served in the army. He was one of the fortunate ones to survive the war, although he carried the injuries sustained in battle, for the rest of his life.

THE 1926 GENERAL STRIKE

The tough economic times following the first World War, and a continuing antipathy against the colliery owners, provided the background to a country-wide coal industry dispute that enveloped the Rhondda in the mid-1920's. Some one million coal miners had been locked out of their mines after a dispute with the owners, who wanted them to work longer hours for less money. In solidarity, the T.U.C. called a general strike on 3rd May. A.J. Cook, a trade unionist, coined the phrase, 'not a penny off the pay, not a minute on the day'. Huge numbers from other industries stayed off work, including bus, rail and dock workers, and those in iron and steel. The aim was to force the government to act to prevent mine owners reducing miners' wages by 13% and increasing their shifts from seven to eight hours. However, nine days after it began, the TUC, which had been holding secret talks with the mine owners, called off the strike without a single concession made to the miners' case. Everyone was taken by surprise, and those strikers from other industries drifted back to work. The miners however, struggled on alone but by the end of six months, most were back down the mines, working longer hours for less pay. Others remained unemployed for many years. It left a bitter taste in the mouth of those of the coal-mining community.

THE 1939/45 SECOND WORLD WAR

World War II was a conflict that involved a large part of the world during the years 1939–45. On the one side it was mainly the forces of Germany, Italy, and Japan; and on the other, the forces of Great Britain, France, the United States, and the Soviet Union, supplemented by those from the Commonwealth countries, etc. The numbers of those who lost their lives were exceptionally large and included many from the Welsh valleys.

It is obvious that, in a period of only 50 years, such a catalogue of events (that included mining disasters, and two world wars, with the attendant austerity, coupled with multiple days, weeks and even months of work lost due to strikes and disputes) would impact greatly on the residents of the Rhondda. My grandparents, parents, and to a much lesser degree myself, lived through this half century. This then, is the background to my early upbringing.

CHAPTER TWO

SOME BIOGRAPHICAL NOTES

TOM (DAD), MY GRAND-FATHER

The head of the house was my grandfather, Thomas James Sheldon (Tom). He was born in 1890. A collier, he married Dorothy (Dolly) Evans. They had four children; Thora, the oldest, was born in December 1910; Billy, in January 1915; then Iris in September 1916 and finally Beryl in March 1920. When my father was born they lived at 61 Ystrad Road, Pentre and Tom worked in a local colliery. His occupation is listed as 'coal hewer' on

Tom is seated on the right

my father's birth certificate. He left the pit to join the Royal Welsh Fusiliers, whether as a volunteer or a conscript I am not sure. While on service in France during the 1914/18 war, he received a battlefield promotion to sergeant. Then, after being wounded, he was shipped home and discharged. His injuries flared up regularly throughout his life and he was often admitted to a military hospital in Llandaff, Cardiff, for treatment. I never remember him without his walking stick on which he leaned heavily.

Trying to make a living was never easy in the valley. No longer able to work in the colliery because of his war injuries, Tom tried his hand at the green-grocery business. He had a stall, under cover, on Pentre Hill, where he was assisted by Dolly, as well as my father.

Tom is on the right, Dolly behind the stall (centre), and my father is the small boy in the front.

They also opened a general shop in the front-room of their home in Churchfield Row, Pentre, after which they resumed the fruit and vegetable business from a shop on the main street in Pentre. This last venture didn't survive the general strike of 1926, because my grandparents gave credit to striking miners

14

which ultimately, they were unable to repay. Tom then tried his hand at selling fruit and vegetables around the terraced streets, from a cart pulled by a very patient horse, but it could never be a long-term occupation. In the 1930s they took responsibility for the Llewellyn Arms Public House. My grand-father was the tenant landlord of the 'Llews' until the mid-1940's.

My memories of grand-father were mostly post-war, that is, post WW2. It seemed then to my young mind, that he had two sides to his character. At home, nothing pleased him. He could always find something to complain about. But when he was out, which was most evenings, he was the life and soul of the party.

He could play the piano, and was much in demand in the local drinking establishments – the British Legion and the Griffin Hotel. Keep him supplied with ale and he would play all the latest hits for sing-songs that went on 'till closing time. He died in June 1965 at the age of 75.

DOLLY (MAM), MY GRAND-MOTHER

Tom's wife, my grand-mother, was a remarkable woman. She came from West Wales, born in Haverfordwest in 1891. Not only raising her own four children, she also took full responsibility for two grand-children (Len and myself). She cooked, cleaned the house, did the washing and the shopping, all duties that were difficult in houses that were cold, draughty, without electricity and very little comfort, in times of austerity. It seemed she was always engaged in duties that might provide some extra income; but too generous of heart to be a success at it.

Shopping, with which I helped when old enough, was particularly difficult, even after the second world war had ended, rationing continued through the 1940's and up to 1954. You queued in the butcher's and the grocer's and still came home with a very light shopping basket. Once a week I was required to walk from Carne Street in Pentre, to Prospect Place in Treorchy, to a small shop where my father and I were still registered to buy groceries. During rationing you had to register with a retailer and then could only use your ration coupons with the one with whom you were

16

registered. I would carry home a shopping bag in which were carefully weighed out amounts of butter, sugar, tea, etc. I suppose we could have re-registered with a shop nearer home, but I was happy to do the journey every week. The owner of the business showed her appreciation of our loyalty by giving me a small individual pot of jam each time.

In a mining valley, cleaning house was no picnic. When you have coal fires; furniture, window sills, mantelpieces and ledges all had to be constantly dusted. In addition, stone floors had to be scrubbed, the grate 'black-leaded' and the front step 'stoned'. All duties that were extremely physical, several of which were performed while on your knees. However, the radio provided a small diversion. It was piped in by Rediffusion, a cable company that provided radio for those areas where reception was either poor or non-existent. My favourites were 'Dick Barton, Special Agent' and 'The Goons', while Mam would not miss her daily dose of 'Mrs. Dales' Diary'. We all listened to programmes like 'Saturday Night Theatre', 'Paul Temple' and especially 'Two Way Family Favourites' on a Sunday lunchtime. In the evenings Mam would knit or sew or repair clothes, and sometimes make rug mats. With a piece of sacking, a special tool with a hook on, and strips of material from worn-out clothes she would fashion rugs to cover the stone floor of the living room and the tiled floor of the passage. She died in 1958, aged 67.

BILL, MY FATHER (DADDY)

He was born in 1915. His childhood was not easy. His father, my grandfather, having been invalided out of the army was trying to make a living in the green-grocery business. In the late 1920's he had a green-grocer's 'round' and travelled up and down the terraced streets selling fruit and vegetables from a horse and cart. He was a severe task master and my father's duties, even as a young schoolboy, included feeding the horse and loading the cart. Sacks of potatoes, nets of onions, boxes of apples, etc. were stacked neatly around the sides of the cart, and the heavy metal scales for weighing produce was placed at the back. Only when he had finished his duties could he go to school. Consequently, he was late every day, and every time he was late, he was 'caned'.

A young Bill Sheldon

Not once was he asked, 'why are you late?' At one stage, my father ran away from home but only got as far as Pontypridd. He had slept in a field and breakfasted on turnips!

In 1928, two years after the general strike of 1926, when he was 13 he was pulled out of school, even though school leaving age was 14. This was so that he could earn money and contribute to family living expenses. It was intended that he 'go down the pit', but that was not permitted until he received his 'school-leaving certificate', which would not be issued until he reached 14 years of age. Tom, found him a job near home, helping in a pawn-shop owned by a well-known local Jewish family. But then, when my father reached age 14, my grand-father insisted he join most of the Rhondda male population in the collieries, descending in cages to the depths of the earth to mine for 'black gold'. His first period in the pit lasted seven years until 1936. This was followed by a short period when he was away from the valley for two years.

Then, on returning to the Rhondda in 1938, he resumed employment at the Parc Colliery as an underground repairer. Always politically conscious he considered himself a Communist. He was secretary of the local miners' 'lodge' and sold the Daily Worker at the pit-head. The newspapers for our house were the Daily Worker and the Soviet Weekly. However, he became disillusioned with Communism after the Soviet invasion of Hungary when they put down the Hungarian uprising in 1956. He died in 2004, aged 89.

Phyllis, My Mother

My mother

My mother was a 'Morris' from Treorchy. She and my father met at a dance, had a whirlwind romance and married in 1934. As a young couple, they 'emigrated' to England to experience life away from the collieries. I was born in Watford in 1937. But my mother had a weak constitution, and was also home-sick; they returned to Treorchy in 1938 to be near her mother and sister. On their return to the Rhondda, my mother resumed her previous occupation – nursing - but it did not last. She was taken ill with tuberculosis and lived the end of her life in Dumfries Street, Treorchy, at the home of her mother. They put a bed for her in the downstairs front room. I visited her each day. Although I was very young, only four years of age, I could travel safely between Prospect Place and Dumfries Street because I did not have to cross any busy roads. On the day she died, I went to visit as usual but was met by members of the Morris family. They clearly did not know how to break the news to a young boy. I was told, 'the gypsies have taken her away'. What a thing to tell a small boy! This is the only lasting memory I have that relates to my mother!

She 'passed away' on the 18th July 1941, aged 27. Her funeral was a sight to behold (or so I'm told). The cortege, with the funeral director walking in front, left Prospect Place, following the side streets until they emerged on the wide main road by the Red Cow Hotel. Turning up the valley and followed on foot by a crowd of mourners, which included those of the nursing fraternity and the fire service, they made their way to Treorchy cemetery, where they were joined at the graveside by men from the colliery who had just come off shift – some still in their working clothes and black-faced. The hymn singing, as befits a valley that boasts several choirs, was inspiring. My mother was laid to rest in the Morris family grave.

As far as I can tell, my father broke off all contact with the Morris family after the death of my mother. His relationship with them was never easy, and after the funeral, for reasons unknown to me, took on the characteristics of a family feud. 'Mam Morris' was employed in the ticket office of the Park and Dare Workman's Hall cinema. When I would 'go to the pictures' I would visit her in the ticket office and she would ask; "'Who do you like best, 'Mam Treorchy' or 'Mam Pentre'?" (referring to

Park and Dare Workmen's Hall today

Daddy's mother). I would offer the required reply, 'Mam Treorchy', whereupon I would receive a threepenny bit to spend, and told at which entrance I could find a friendly attendant who would let me in for free if I said the magic sentence, 'Mam sent me'. The threepence would be enough for me to get a choc-ice (my uncle had the ice-cream franchise for the cinema).

The passing of my mother brought to a close an eventful period in the life of my father. In work at age 13; down the pit at 14; married at 19; 'emigrated' to England looking for work at 21; a father at 22; returned to the Rhondda to work underground at 23; and a widower at 26. Times were not easy!

CHAPTER THREE

THE EARLY YEARS

To recap, I was born just before the outbreak of the second world war (1937 to be precise). My father (William Thomas Sheldon) and mother (Phyllis Dwynwen Sheldon née Morris) were from the Rhondda but were living in Watford at the time, where my father was employed as a green-grocer's assistant. We returned to the Rhondda in 1938, partly because my mother was not strong, and partly because she missed her family. On our return, we took residence in a terraced house in Prospect Place and my father obtained employment in the Parc Colliery as an underground road repairer. He had worked in the pits from the age of 14 so was fully familiar with the work. With the outbreak of war in 1939 those involved in the production of coal were declared to be in essential and protected employment, so my father continued in the Parc Pit until 1953. He left after the regulations were eased.

After the decease of my mother, we went to live with my grand-parents (Tom and Dolly Sheldon) in the Llewellyn Arms Public House in Pentre. My grand-father was the tenant landlord of the 'Llews' which was a tied house. Owned by a brewery, he could only sell those products supplied by the brewery owners. The premises were large and full of wonder for a young boy. There were loads of rooms and cellars to explore and a stable out back which fascinated me. Enough room for everyone. The occupants were Tom and Dolly (Mam and Dad); then their children, Bill (my father), Iris, Beryl and Len, and lastly me as the only grandchild at that time. Iris and Beryl were married but their husbands, Frank and Jim were away in the armed forces. After the war, when the men returned to 'civvy street', Iris and Frank moved to London while Beryl and Jim set up home locally (in Ton-Pentre). I cannot remember Thora, the oldest of Tom and Dolly's children. I have the impression that she had married and moved to another valley, but I am unable to confirm that.

Our time at the Llewellyn's did not last long. My grand-father, with another local pub landlord, was trying to make a little extra money on   the side by selling 'black-market' whisky. However, he was discovered when a representative of the brewery paid him an unexpected visit. Tom was given a choice – leave quietly or face prosecution. He left quietly. We moved to 14 Carne Street, Pentre.

LIFE IN CARNE STREET

Our new home was spacious enough for us. It had three bedrooms. The front bedroom for my father and myself – the middle bedroom for Tom and Dolly – and the back bedroom for my uncle Len, who deserves an extra mention. He was Thora's boy (which would make him my cousin). But Thora, my father's sister, had had Len out of

14 Carne Street

wedlock and, as was often the custom then, he was adopted by her mother and father (Tom and Dolly) to 'give him a name' and minimise the shame. This meant that he went from being my cousin to my uncle, Len suddenly becoming my father's younger brother.

I was still very young when we moved to Carne Street. A main road terraced property, it was very primitive, even for the war years. It had no electricity or hot water and no bathroom (these conditions lasted for several years). The toilet was located at the end of the garden and on bath nights a tin bath was utilised. The water for bathing was heated in a galvanised bucket over the coal fire in the living room. It was some time before we got a gas boiler to heat the water. There were pithead baths for the men working at the collieries (Daddy and Len) but my weekly bath took place in front of the fire in the living room.

The coal fire was the centre part of a three-section iron unit comprising of an oven to the left of the fire, and on the right, a water holder to provide a ready supply of hot water (although I never remember it being used, probably because it leaked). The oven was used for a variety of purposes, including drying out the sticks needed to light the fire.

We made the best of life in Carne Street. It was a big day when electricity was put in for the first time. But my grandfather did not spend money very easily and it was limited to two ceiling lights downstairs and one socket outlet. My duties continued to contain the changing of gas mantles! It was some years later that the house was fully electrified.

The ground floor consisted of a front room which, in common with many a Rhondda home, contained a glass cabinet with a bone china tea service. Apart from funerals, front rooms in the valley were rarely used. But at times of bereavement, it was the room which housed the coffin.

Next on the ground floor was the 'living room', which was usually called the 'middle room', and was the heart of the house. Then a kitchen in which there was a gas cooker, and lastly a small addition to the back of the ground floor, a pantry.

The living room had the only fire, which was lit every morning with crumpled newspaper, then a layer of sticks, and placed on top of that, a layer of coal. With two colliery workers in the home we had a ready supply of coal. The back garden was about 20 yards long and on a gradient. It was rarely cultivated. It had a path up the middle, at the end and to the left of which was the coal shed, more familiarly known as the 'coal cwtch'. Opposite the coal shed and to the right of the path was the toilet.

We were fortunate to have a dirt lane outside the back wall which could be negotiated by a coal lorry. Coal was dropped (a ton at a time) in this lane. Len or my father would throw it into the coal cwtch, through a hole in back wall. There was always a residue of 'small coal', more like coal dust, left in the lane after a delivery. This was later collected by a man called 'Dai-small-coal', who made his living by selling it on. Those homes that lacked back lane access had the coal dropped on the road at the front of the house, and it had to be carried, in buckets, through the home to a storage area at the back.

My father and Len brought 'blocks' home from the pit whenever it was 'block day'. One of the perks of working in the colliery was that on 'block day' you could take home two foot-long sections of a wooden pit prop. A heavy axe in the hands of a coal miner could, in no time, reduce these to the size of sticks, suitable for kindling the fire. As I got older I was permitted to wield the axe!

The kitchen had a sink over which was a cold-water tap. This was the only water source inside the house. It had a serious drawback – the pipes that fed it were outside, which meant they froze whenever the temperature dropped, after which they often leaked. But some of the pipes were lead and were easily repaired, that is, when they were accessible, which was not always the case.

Every morning before going to school, I washed my hands and face at the kitchen sink. We used the same green soap for personal ablutions as was used for washing the clothes. On one occasion, Len took offence at something I said and decided I should 'wash my mouth out'. Older and stronger, he forced me bite down on a square of soap, holding my mouth shut for some time! It was hours, perhaps even days, before the appalling taste began to fade.

The pantry had a large stone slab, called 'the cold stone' on which we kept any items of food or drink that needed to be kept cool. The jug of milk was always kept in the pantry – there were no 'fridges' in those days.

The routine of the house was repetitive. Monday was wash-day, Tuesday was ironing day, Wednesday was cleaning day, and so on. To do the weekly wash we had a washing-machine, at least that's what we called it. It was simply a tub on four legs that had an 'agitator' in the lid. The agitator was a paddle that lived inside the tub but had a handle outside the lid.

I remember the days when the water was heated in the bucket on the fire and then poured into the tub. Big green bars of soap were reduced to flakes by using a cheese-grater and scattered in the water. After the dirty clothes had been added to the tub it was necessary to manually 'agitate' the clothes and water, and generate enough soap suds to begin to clean the clothes. Mam would say to me, 'give me a hundred', which meant turn the agitator back and fore one hundred times. Often the clothes would need some extra attention by placing them on a scrubbing board and applying 'elbow-grease'. The 'washing machine' was always used outside in the back yard. Attached to the tub was a mangle, through which you fed the wet clothes to extract as much liquid as possible before pegging them out on the long washing line at the rear of the house. The clothes line was held up by a prop to make best use of the wind. On a wet day, wet washing was draped over wooden clothes-horses around the fire in the living room. The severe limitations we suffered at Carne Street gradually eased over the years. A gas boiler was purchased to heat water so 'the bucket over the fire' was no longer needed – a good thing too, for it was clearly a dangerous practice.

On one side of the living room was an upright piano which had been brought from the 'Llews', on which my grandfather practiced the latest popular songs. Sometimes I would be sent to a local furniture shop which, incongruously, sold sheet music. For one shilling and sixpence you could buy a copy of the latest hit. I always thought they were expensive and the money could have been used for some better purpose. I did not realise that they were an investment for Dad – knowing the latest songs kept him in demand in the local inns.

In the centre of the living room was a table where our meals were eaten. During the war years meat was both expensive and scarce.

Inventive ways were devised to use whatever was available. There were always sausages in the butcher's window, although what was in them I was never sure. They were heavily seasoned and tasted good, so I never asked. On occasion Mam would make tripe and onions. The tripe on sale was the lining from the stomach of cattle. It was highly nutritious (or so I'm told – I never ate it). Sometimes my grandfather would try to help by making home-made brawn. He boiled half a pig's head in a large saucepan over the fire; then extracted all the bits of meat he could. Nothing wasted, he gathered them up in a basin and compressed them under a plate on which a heavy weight from a green-grocer's scales was placed. It came out of the basin in one lump like a jelly out of a mould. When cold, the home-made brawn could be sliced and used in sandwiches, etc.

My grandmother was reduced to opening a 'club' with local retailers to get shoes or clothes on credit. A 'club' was where you bought something, paid a little off the purchase price, with the rest going 'on the book', that is, on credit. Then week by week you would pay off the balance. We had a 'club' for shoes in Morris's in Gelli and a 'club' in Edwards' drapery for clothes. Since we rarely finished paying for something before it needed replacing, or other demands were made on the household budget, we were always in debt. Friday was pay-day, so Saturday would be the day when there would be a knock at the door by someone who was collecting the weekly contribution for the 'shoe-club' or 'clothes club'. Having said that, my grand-mother never let the debts escalate until they were unmanageable. Better to do without than incur debt which could not be repaid!

On one occasion we received a food parcel from Canada, at least that was what it was called. It was a sealed tin box which took some ingenuity even to open. Inside we discovered items such as hard biscuits (which needed a hammer to break) and dried egg powder. There was very little in the tin that was edible. But as they say, it is the thought that counts! It was several years after the war ended before items that were considered luxuries, like chocolate and bananas, became available. I still remember my first taste of Rollo (it was heavenly).

WHAT ABOUT SCHOOL?

Up to the age of eleven I attended Pentre Junior School. It was at the top of a very steep hill, but hills had never been a problem for me. Living in the valley and always near a mountain, climbing steep slopes presented no difficulty.

My free time was mostly spent on a mountain, which was considered 'safe' in those days.

Each week day I would rise, wash, dress and make myself breakfast (usually a jam sandwich) and go to school. I remember one particular day when I followed the usual routine. When I arrived in the school yard there was no-one there, which was not unusual (I was often early). I lingered for a while, kicking a ball about to pass the time, until it began to dawn on me that there was something wrong. There was – it was a Sunday! When I got home, there were no awkward questions to face - I hadn't been missed.

I enjoyed school – we had a popular teacher and the subjects were not demanding. On the other hand, being under-weight, I was easy fodder for bullies and after school each day, one brute of a boy would twist my arm behind my back and march me to his house. I was only released after I acknowledged his superiority. By this time, I accepted such things as a part of life – to be suffered without complaint. I had no ambitions and very little expectation of happiness.

I always enjoyed the holiday breaks from school, especially during the summer. I was away from the daily 'bullying' and I also had freedom to wander the mountains and explore

Pentre woods. We never took a family holiday together, although there was always a two-week period in the summer that was called 'miners' fortnight'. Many families from the valley rented a caravan in Trecco Bay, Porthcawl. They might have had a change in location, but somehow ended up with the same neighbours!

The end of the war in 1945 gave the community reasons to celebrate, and street parties were organised. Long lines of tables were placed in the road, and everyone brought a cup, saucer and plate, together with a knife and spoon. We feasted on cup-cakes, jelly and blancmange; and washed it all down with pop from Thomas and Evans.

Out of school I joined in such games that children my age played. Mostly street games like 'kick the tin'; 'catty and doggy', and after it was dark, 'hide and seek'. Those with a more adventurous nature joined the 'jazz bands'. These were groups of children aged from 8 to 16, who were trained to march in unison to the beat of a drum. Mothers made brightly coloured uniforms for them to wear, and competitions were held with prizes for the band that not only looked good but performed the best marching programme. The bands were mostly comprised of girls, with a few boy drummers in the rear, tapping out the beat on kettle drums, together with one boy big enough to carry the big, booming, bass drum. The bands were always led by a baton-twirling majorette. The children played kazoos while on the march. It all served to provide an attractive diversion to the mundane daily routine of life in the valley. Competitions were held on the rugby field in Treorchy. It was a venue that was used for a variety of public events, including athletics and speedway racing.

With the loss of my mother I no longer had a family. I lived in the same house as my father and my grandparents, but did not feel a member of the family. I was barely tolerated by my grandfather and mostly ignored by my father whom I rarely saw. He worked nights and slept part of the day. At weekends, he went out to social events - some dance halls had re-opened and there was always a dance to go to (for example, at Judges' Hall, Tonypandy, the Library in Llwynypia or the British Legion in Pentre). With two colliery workers in the house there should have been enough money coming into the house to meet the needs of all, but the three men, Tom, Len and my father, were all smokers and drinkers and given to a hectic, expensive, social life, so my needs were mostly overlooked.

Nicknames

My father's best friend was another coal-miner called Joe Sol. I assumed that Sol was short for Solomon, which could have been his middle name or perhaps his surname. It turned out to be neither. His name was Joe Morgan, but since there were also other 'Joe Morgans' he was identified as Joe Sol, because his father was Solomon Morgan, i.e. Joe, was the son of Solomon Morgan – therefore 'Joe Sol'. Names were never what they seemed in the valley. Nicknames were plentiful. 'Dai-small-coal' we have already mentioned. 'Dai the oil', had a hardware shop in Treorchy, but received his nickname because he also sold paraffin oil from the back of a van. I was told of 'Dai-central-'eating', who had his name because he only had one tooth in the middle of his mouth, and 'Dai-six-months' because he only had half an ear (although I think these last two were apocryphal). My father told me of an Englishman who settled in the Rhondda and came to work at the Parc Colliery. He tried to pre-empt the Welsh habit of allocating nicknames and said, 'If you have to give me a nickname, make it sedate'. Thereafter he was called 'Dai-sedate'. I never worked out why they were always called 'Dai'. The shops in Pentre did not have nick-names but were identified in a peculiarly Welsh way. Shops like 'Harris the

Barbers', 'Phillips the Typewriters', 'Morris the Butchers', 'Edwards the Drapers', and 'Morris the Shoes'.

HEALTH CARE PRIOR TO THE NHS

There were two main surgeries in Treorchy. One served by Dr. Fergus Armstrong and one by a Dr. Morris. We were registered with Dr. Morris. If you needed medication you visited their surgery. There were never enough doctors servicing the valley and you would always be met by a long queue. Surgery opening times were limited and often there would be patients waiting outside for the doors to open. Waiting rooms were bare and uninviting, with wooden benches around the walls. It was a 'sit-down' queue and everyone moved along one place as someone was seen by the doctor.

In 1948, I developed appendicitis. Our family doctor was Dr. Morris. He recommended surgery and I was admitted to 'Pentwyn Cottage Hospital'. It had been built in 1924 for the colliery workers and maintained by their weekly subscriptions, which included the services of Dr. Armstrong, who had the reputation of being an exceptional surgeon. However, I was Dr. Morris' patient, so he performed the operation. My appendectomy

Pentwyn Cottage Hospital

was successful (I still have the scar) but Dr. Morris was very cautious, and I remained in hospital for almost five weeks. While there, we were provided with a constant supply of water, drawn from a well in the grounds. It was always ice-cold and better tasting than that which gurgled out of the tap at home.

'Mam' was the one to keep an eye on my health. From the earliest time my well-being had been delegated to her, adding to her already full and busy life, but over the years she was less able to care for others. Gradually going blind (cataracts I think it was) I had to look after myself as best I could. Many of the small ailments I suffered as a child were simply the result of a poor immune system due to under-nourishment and a poor diet. In the earlier years, I had lived on bread and jam and free school meals. Later, I learned to cook simple meals, but I was always under-weight. At 18 years of age I still was only 8 stone.

CHAPTER FOUR

THE TEEN YEARS

PORTH COUNTY GRAMMAR SCHOOL

I passed the eleven-plus exams (23rd for Pentre Secondary School and 33rd in the Rhondda for Porth County Grammar School) despite having been absent from lessons while in hospital. It was customary for success at the exams to be rewarded with a gift. While others received a bike, my father gave me a small compass. It was a big disappointment!

My time at 'Porth County Grammar' was not happy. I was out of my depth in so many ways. The one unfortunate consequence of my early upbringing was that it left me with no social skills, and low self-esteem; limitations which have beset me all my life.

On attending grammar school at 12 years of age I was soon marked out as someone who came from poverty. My grandmother, who did her best to clothe me, could not afford the school uniform (green blazer and grey trousers), so I wore my everyday clothes with just a school badge sown on to my jacket. I was not the only one, of course, but it did not lessen my chagrin.

Discipline was severe, and it now seems to me that many of the Masters enjoyed dispensing corporal punishment. They had canes that liked the taste of young boys' flesh. One used a 'dap' (plimsole) on the buttocks. Allan Jones sat opposite me in class and on one occasion we were caught talking to each other. We were hit around the head with a text book, while the teacher hummed the opening bars of the 'Anvil Chorus', ensuring his blows were in time with the music.

Grammar school did produce some beneficial effects though. I excelled at English and Maths without really trying, and I discovered I was better than most at sport. In the summer, I, along with others from 'County' played cricket. At weekends, and sometimes in the long summer evenings, we played on the Treorchy Washery. It was a remnant of a colliery washery that once served the Abergorki Colliery which had closed in 1938. It suited us because the coal dust had compacted into a fairly level playing surface. In addition, there were the ruins of buildings still around where we could shelter if it rained, and since we were in a Welsh valley, that was a regular occurrence. The big drawback, of course, was that we were as black as the ace of spades after a session on our 'small-coal' pitch.

In the winter, it was football. One of the regular football pitches was on 'the target', a field sited at the top of the mountain overlooking Cwmparc and Treorchy. It had one major drawback. Any errant strike of the ball and it went tumbling down the mountain and the game had to be suspended until someone went down to retrieve it (we usually only had one football!)

I never made any close friends although there were one or two at school that I felt comfortable with. Peter Davies was one – a boy with impeccable manners, and excellent social skills. Allan Jones was another – a sprinter who could run like the wind. He would have been schools champion but for one weakness – he was slow out of the blocks!

LOW-KEY ADVENTURES FOR A TEENAGER

In my mid-teens, I needed a new jacket, so Mam took me to Edwards' Drapery on Pentre Hill. It was a haberdasher's and milliner's as well as a draper's. Mainly for women, it had a small section for men and boys. The visit was excruciatingly embarrassing for me. I was served by a very attractive young woman. Taking her opportunity to have a little fun at my expense she smiled and reached around me to take my chest measurement. I had never been that close to a female in my life before, so

43

I was soon reduced to a stuttering, blushing, piece of jelly. And even after suffering such an ordeal I was left with a choice of only two coats, neither of which were 'fashionable', and only one which was a reasonable fit. But beggars can't be choosers and I went home, the possessor of a 'salt and pepper' jacket and a little wiser!

In those days, among the men, smoking was almost universal. Some were chain-smokers, lighting the next cigarette from the expiring one. I was saved from acquiring the habit by a small, insignificant event. Our milk was delivered each day by a young man who brought it in a small churn. Sometimes I would be the one to go to the front door with an enamel jug and ask for 'a pint of milk, please'. He, using a half-pint measuring ladle, would pour the milk into our jug. But he had a quick hand and never allowed the milk to come to rest, so I doubt if we ever received full measure for our money. One day he arrived with a cigarette in his lips, and asked me if I smoked. I replied in the negative, whereupon he offered me his cigarette for a drag. I took a small puff and offered it back. He said I should take a proper pull on the cigarette and 'take it down', that is, breathe it in. I did so and started to cough so loudly that it disturbed my father who was in bed in the front bed-room. I coughed for what seemed an eternity and until I ached. I never was tempted by the tobacco leaf again. The men of the family, though, smoked anything from Woodbines to Capstan Full Strength (otherwise known as 'coffin nails'). My grandfather bought Players cigarettes by the carton. On one occasion, to gain acceptance with a local gang, I stole some cigarettes from his stash, thinking he wouldn't miss them. He did, and I got into real trouble!

CHAPTER FIVE

SOCIAL LIFE IN THE VALLEY

The social life of the valley was dominated by pubs and clubs. At that time, the clubs had a slight edge over the pubs because of the licensing laws. From 1881 until 2003 the pubs in Wales closed on a Sunday. Nevertheless, they were popular during the week. Those that gambled would visit the pub to place a bet with the bookie's runner, and of course, have a pint of best Welsh Bitter at the same time. No printed betting slips, of course. A couple of bob each way on your chosen horse (or some such bet) was written on any scrap of paper, including the back of cigarette packets and, together with the stake, passed surreptitiously to the runner sitting in the corner of a local hotel. When the law changed in 1961 and betting shops were opened, the whole dynamic changed.

Pubs also had a darts team which would play in a local league. When I was in my early 20's I played darts for the Stag Hotel on a Friday, and the Pengelli Hotel on a Wednesday – although I was not very good. But the purpose was mainly to have fun and not worry about winning.

Another limitation of the public houses was their clientele was mostly men. It was the clubs that began to welcome the women. And there were clubs everywhere: workmen's clubs, rugby clubs, clubs for the unemployed; even clubs for the main political parties. Every village had its 'Conservative Club' and 'Labour Club', and sometimes even a 'Liberal Club', although it would be impossible to find anyone in the valley who would confess to being a Liberal, or a Conservative for that matter.

The workmen's halls provided a valuable service. Most had a snooker hall, and all had a library. Many miners would spend time at the library focusing on subjects that they were interested in. Even some who had never received a formal education excelled in specialist disciplines. I learned very early that you never argued with a miner. He might be dressed in well-worn clothes and have the appearance of an uneducated man, but you might discover that you are dealing with an expert in the field.

There would be others who would use their leisure hours looking after pigeons. Dotted along the hillsides of the valley, from Porth to Blaenrhondda were pigeon coops painted in 'black and white' squares – easily spotted by the racing pigeon when 'homing'. Baskets of the birds would be sent by rail to regular destinations, where the station staff would liberate them and then return the empty baskets on the next available train. Many champion racing pigeons were bred in the Rhondda.

Then there were the bands and the choirs. As with other mining areas, the Rhondda had its share of brass bands, some quite well known such as the 'Cory Band' and the 'Parc and Dare Band'. They entered national competitions and often were successful. So too, the choirs; Treorchy boasted a large, male-voice choir that often won first prize at Eisteddfods. The choirs were mostly 'men only' although there were one or two that were mixed.

WHAT ABOUT GIRLS?

The grammar school I attended served the Rhondda. It was divided into two, with a fence between. On the lower side of the fence was the boy's school, and on the upper side of the fence was the girl's school. The playgrounds for the two schools were close together, which meant we could see the girls, but they might just as well have been miles away – there was no social contact. But after school – well, that was another matter! But my social skills were almost non-existent, and although I dipped my toes into the water a couple of times and invited a girl or two out, nothing clicked – I was too much of a novice. But I was a tryer and my abilities improved with practice. One evening, on a visit to the local cinema I met up with a girl with whom I was acquainted. We talked and walked. Soon I had a girl-friend. The relationship took some time to blossom and would be dented when I was called up for national service – but, after some six years we would fully commit to each other and marry.

Maureen and Me (c. 1954)

CHAPTER SIX

LIFE AFTER SCHOOL

'O' LEVELS

Drawing near to school leaving age I was required first to sit the 'O' level examinations. I never studied much and never revised for exams, and so expectations were not high. With Maths and English I had no trouble, and I could cope with Physics (there was a Maths component to the subject), but everything else was a relative mystery to me.

I did manage to get a pass in Metalwork though. We were required to make a hasp and eye that would receive a lock and could be screwed onto wooden doors or gates. We were given a metal rod that needed to be bent into shape to serve as the 'eye'. I made a mess of mine and went, rather sheepishly, to the visiting invigilating master to explain. He took the rod from me and began to fashion it saying, 'if you did this it would look better'. By the time he had finished I had the best hasp and eye in the room and passed the exam with flying colours. However, having 'metalwork' on your C.V. does not open many doors! So, I left school at 16 with only 4 'O' level passes – Maths, English, Physics and Metalwork.

WHEN MY FATHER LEFT

When it happened I do not know, but my father reconnected with Maisie, a woman he had known before he married my mother. She lived in a bed-sit in Cardiff and worked for Vernon's Pools, so he travelled each weekend to see her. They could not marry because she had a husband – she was separated but not divorced. She also had a son, but it seems he did not feature in her plans in the same way as I did not feature in my father's plans.

During the war years Maisie had been employed as a companion and personal help to a wealthy Jewish woman who had been evacuated from the London area. The husband had remained in Staines, in Surrey, where he had a factory that made clothes. During the war years he was contracted to make uniforms for the military. After the war, the family re-united in Staines. They maintained contact with Maisie and Daddy and offered my father a job in the clothing factory in Staines. It was about 1953 and the embargo on men leaving the mines had been lifted, so he accepted their offer and made plans to leave the Rhondda. I knew nothing of this until I was called before him for a special talk. Placed before me were two alternatives. The first - to join him and Maisie in Surrey where we would live together in a static caravan on a site located near the Thames. Or I could stay and live with Mam in Carne Street. Expected to make an immediate decision, I had a sense that staying was the option he hoped I would choose, so I chose to stay. A few days later my father had gone. I had little contact with him again until the age of 20.

The first consequence of my father's departure was that I lost my bedroom. It was the largest bedroom and had the best furniture – furniture that was new when my parents married. We brought a bedroom suite with us after my mother's decease. But now with my father gone, I was relegated to the back bedroom: it was a small room with one very old double bed that nearly filled it. No space for extra furniture. How Len had managed there I will never understand. My move to the back-bedroom seemed an omen to me. It just confirmed what I already knew – I was at the bottom of the pecking order!

EMPLOYMENT FOR A SCHOOL LEAVER

After I left school I needed employment. I reported to the job centre and got a position with the Treorchy Co-op as a milkman's assistant. A team of two, we had a round that covered Cwmparc, Treorchy and Treherbert, a particularly large section of the Rhondda where many streets were built on the side of mountains. This meant it was particularly demanding, especially on the driver's assistant – me! We had one of those electric delivery trucks which was loaded each morning with crates of milk. The loaded vehicle was unable to climb the hill-side streets that were the main part of our route, so the driver stayed with the milk-float on the main road, and I was given two hand crates to fill and carry up the hills to customers living in the side streets. I would fill my hand crates from a reserve of larger crates that had been dropped off at a convenient street corner and then climb hill after hill after hill! It was exhausting! To make it worse, it seemed it was always raining. My uncle had provided me with some oilskins to wear in bad weather. While they kept out the rain they were exceptionally heavy and hot to wear. I looked like a North Sea fisherman in them. Due to perspiration, it was as wet under the waterproofs as it was outside them!

Each morning we would stop for breakfast at Ernie's café in Treorchy where I would be treated to tea and toast. My driver always took the money from the bag where he kept customer's payments, so I never knew whether I was being 'treated' by the milkman, or it was considered one of the 'perks' of the job. After a couple of days of rising at 5 a.m. and exploring every street from Cwmparc to Treherbert I concluded – 'this job is not for me' – I finished the week, got my pay and then resigned.

EMPLOYMENT ON THE RAILWAY

In the absence of my father, my uncle Len decided to take a hand in getting me my next job. We visited our local independent counsellor, Glyn Wales, who was employed at Ystrad Railway Station. He drafted a letter for me, and I used it to apply for a job with British Railways. When interviewed, it seemed four 'O' levels were more than enough to be employed as a booking clerk. I was to be employed at Tonyrefail station on the Ely line. I was told to report to Penygraig railway station where I would meet the station master (he was in charge of all the stations on the Ely branch line) and then take the train to Tonyrefail, the next station on the line.

On getting the appointment, I was totally bemused. I thought the only railway line in the Rhondda ran along the floor of the valley and Penygraig was way up the mountain, as is inferred by its name (Pen (top) Graig (rock)). On my first day I rose early, dressed in such clothes as would befit a clerk, and took the bus to Penygraig to search for the railway station. Near the main road I discovered a sign pointing further up the mountain. It read, 'To the station'. I climbed the hill and found it at last.

From its entrance, it had a glorious view of the valley which stretched out below. When I walked onto the platform it seemed as if I had turned back the clock. It was 1953, yet the station had no electricity – light was provided by gas lamps, which were ignited by a pilot light when you pulled on a chain attached to a lever that opened the gas jet. The platform itself had a timber section that was no longer safe and had been fenced off. While it had a certain charm, it did seem left over from a different era.

The station master came out from his office to meet me. His uniform had seen better days and he was quite small, about five feet tall. I would have guessed he was over sixty years of age and near retirement. He asked me where I had attended school. When I said 'Porth County' he replied his son also had gone to 'County'. When he gave me his son's name I gasped in amazement. The boy in question had been several years ahead of me and was a giant, heavy set and well over six feet tall. With the problem of the age gap and the difference in size between father and son I think he must have been adopted, but I never got the courage to ask.

The station master rolled his own cigarettes, but since he also had 'the shakes' it ended with more tobacco on the floor than in the Rizla.

Somehow it did not seem out of place. Even the train I was to take to travel to my home station, Tonyrefail, seemed to be a relic of an earlier time. It comprised of two carriages pulled by a steam engine that pulled the carriages up the valley and did the return journey pushing from behind.

Everything about the Ely line was quite informal. Regular passengers from Penygraig were few (considering the climb up the mountain to get to the station it was a wonder there were any!) There was only one season ticket holder. A quite lovely young woman who was early each morning and always invited into the office for a cup of tea and a seat by the coal fire. One morning she was late. The guard, who always looked forward to her company on the short journey to Llantrisant, held the train for a minute or two but when there was no sign of her called the 'all clear'. The train started to pull out of the station with the guard looking back to see if she would appear. Just as it cleared the platform she came breathlessly into sight. The train driver, who was also aware of the situation braked and then reversed back to the platform to pick her up. Now that's the kind of service you got on the Ely line! I was told that the driver made up the time before he reached Llantrisant, so no need to put any of those details into his logbook.

The Ely line had only five passenger trains each day. Two in the morning, sometimes with a guard's van full of produce for local merchants, and often pulling a couple of goods wagons loaded with fruit and vegetables for the local wholesalers (these would be shunted into a siding for unloading). Only rarely did they carry any passengers. But in Penygraig, the trains would change lines and return to pick up office workers travelling from Tonyrefail to Llantrisant. In Llantrisant, passengers could disembark and take a main-line train to Cardiff. The third of the five trains came at lunch time, and another two in the evening bringing the office workers back.

However, during the summer a mighty change took place. At the weekends, excursions were run to Porthcawl, a seaside town with excellent beaches and an amusement park. Fares were attractively priced, and hundreds of passengers would invade the station. From the booking office window, there was a view of an adjacent field, in the middle of which was a path coming from the direction of Gilfach Goch. Some twenty minutes before the train was due to leave, there still would be large numbers of parents with animated children, carrying bags containing sandwiches and Corona pop, coming across the field; all eagerly anticipating a rare treat – a day out at the seaside. Even with extra carriages I often doubted we would get everyone on board, but somehow, we always did.

Apart from a porter, I would often be on duty on my own, to 'book the train'. There would be never-ending queues of people asking for 'one and three halves', meaning one adult and three children, or something similar. Each ticket had to be date stamped and child tickets (the halves) were literally half a ticket, that is, an adult ticket obliquely cut in half. I had a fares ready reckoner on the wall, a scissors to hand, and a mountain of change, but it was very demanding, and the train rarely left on time. I would breathe a sigh of relief when I balanced the cash at the end of the shift.

One of the duties I was happy to embrace was doing the monthly accounts. At the end of each month we were required to balance all revenues and send in our returns. With my aptitude for anything to do with figures I found it both easy and enjoyable.

While I was mainly employed to deal with passenger traffic, coal traffic was also part of my remit. The Ely line was mostly used for coal traffic. Long lines of empty coal trucks would travel up the valley to Cambrian Colliery which was situated at the top of Clydach Vale (beyond Penygraig station), before returning fully loaded on the way to fuel power stations and industry. Similarly, journeys of coal trucks would travel up a branch line to the Britannic Colliery in Gilfach Goch, while others turned into the sidings at Coedely Colliery, further down the valley. Regularly, I caught a bus from Tonyrefail to Gilfach, to the station building situated at the side of the main road. There I would fill in wagon returns, listing coal traffic activity over the previous twenty-four hours. I travelled by bus for these duties because there were no passenger trains running up the Gilfach valley. For months I had been under the impression that the Gilfach line had been built for coal traffic only. It was somewhat of a revelation when I was informed that, years before, there had been a regular passenger service serving those who lived at the top of the valley. The platform where passengers entrained and alighted was 'hidden' behind a wall. It had remained undiscovered by me for some time because it could not be seen from the office and to get to it you walked over 'sleepers' laid between the rails.

One day, to my surprise, I was asked to book an excursion that was to start at Gilfach. It would pick up more passengers at Coedely and Llantrisant before travelling on to Porthcawl. I thought someone was pulling my leg, but it was true, and when the day arrived crowds of people squeezed onto the short platform before being shepherded on to the 'seaside express'. After the departure of the excursion I cashed up and returned to my home station by bus!

OTHER DUTIES

With so few passenger trains I filled up my time with other duties. The parcel office was always busy – parcel traffic was quite healthy, so some days I would help there – other times I would join the delivery driver on his rounds. I got to know nearly all the streets in Gilfach and Tonyrefail. Other days I would join one of the porters in cleaning oil lamps to replace those in the signals that were low on oil. I was never allowed to climb to the high oil lamps so had to content myself with the ground signals.

PAYING THE WORKERS

There were many workers that had a part in keeping the line going. Besides the station master, the chief clerk, and the booking clerk (me), there were the porters, the delivery drivers, the signal-men, the brake-men, as well as the permanent-way men. All had to be paid and one of my duties was to prepare the paybill. It would be sent to the main office in Cardiff to be checked and then the money for the wages would be sent by train for us to make up the wage packets. However, since there were so few trains coming up the Ely line, none of which began in Cardiff, it had been decided to send the wages via the Rhondda Valley line and we were to collect it from Tonypandy station. This called for a bus journey from Tonyrefail to Tonypandy once a week. I was delegated to the duty and given a porter as a security guard. I wore a trench coat with large 'poacher's pockets' in which to hide the leather pouch which contained the week's wages for the whole workforce of the Ely line. If anyone had decided to rob us it would have been like taking candy from a baby. Nevertheless, week after week I carried the money back to Tonyrefail to be made up into pay packets for the men.

My time at Tonyrefail station was quite a happy one. I was engaged in a job I could perform without too many problems. However, my 18th birthday was on the horizon and, in the short-term future, national service loomed large. The personnel department of British Railways in Cardiff were aware of it and installed a replacement for me in Tonyrefail, at the same time employing me as a relief booking clerk to cover absenteeism and holidays in other stations. My life began to be somewhat more complicated.

CHAPTER SEVEN

LIFE IN THE SERVICE OF HER MAJESTY

One day in 1955, the postman delivered an envelope with the initials O.H.M.S. on it. I was to report to a building in Cardiff for a medical to see if I was healthy enough for duty in Her Majesty's armed forces. Apart from being only eight stone in weight I was quite fit. I could run like the wind and run forever (or so it seemed). I was put through the usual tests, and had to fill out several forms. Everything was going fine until the eye test. There was a card on the wall with several rows of letters. The top row had a large 'A' on it; then rows of random letters underneath which decreased in size little by little. I had to stand by a chalk mark drawn on the wooden floor and read the letters. No problem, I thought. But when a doctor's assistant came behind me with a wooden spoon and used it to cover one of my eyes, the letters on the card quickly became unreadable. This was repeated with the other eye, with the same result. It seemed I needed spectacles. My eyes were out of focus and needed correction. It was a surprise to me, for I had been reading railway timetables with small numbers for a couple of years. But apart from that I was declared fit and suitable for 'call-up'. I visited an optician in Pentre, obtained a pair of spectacles and was suitably amazed at how much more I could see. Something beneficial had resulted from my medical!

The examinations were not only physical. There were written exams also. Various questionnaires and aptitude tests. I had no problems with this part of the day. What shape came next? What number was missing? Fill in the blanks. It seemed I made the grade – it was the R.A.F for me with the possibility of officer training.

LIFE IN THE R.A.F.

In June of that year I was instructed to report to R.A.F. Cardington, a reception camp in Bedfordshire, where I was to be kitted out with the uniforms and accoutrements needed for life in the service. Included with my joining instructions was a railway travel pass. When the day arrived, I made my way to Ystrad Station to catch the appropriate train. On the platform I met up with Billy Jones, a boy who had also attended Porth County Grammar School. Coincidentally, Billy was on his way to R.A.F. Cardington. Suddenly things became a little easier – I had company facing a fairly large change in my life.

At Cardington, Billy and I were in the same billet, and in the relaxed atmosphere of a reception unit, we thought that life in the Air Force wasn't so bad after all. Apart from reporting to various buildings where we received uniforms and kit-bags, etc. our time was our own. There was the NAAFI which was equipped with games rooms; and a free cinema which had a regular change of films. We were being eased into service; but big changes were on the horizon.

On the last day of our time at Cardington, we evacuated our billets in the morning. Wearing our dress uniform and greatcoat, and carrying full kitbags, we were lined up on the parade ground, standing 'at ease', waiting for buses to take us to another camp. We were there for hours in the summer heat. Airmen were dropping to the ground with heat exhaustion. NCOs were walking up and down the ranks advising, 'look into the distance at something green'. When the buses finally came we were on our way to R.A.F. Hednesford in Staffordshire, for eight weeks' basic training, otherwise known as 'square-bashing'.

R.A.F. HEDNESFORD

On arrival at Hednesford we were met by two corporal drill instructors who screamed instructions incessantly. Life in the Air Force had suddenly taken a turn for the worse! Billy and I were separated, and I was billeted with about twenty other recruits. We were a mixed lot – some only 18 years of age, like myself, but a good sprinkling of others who had had their service deferred, that is, their time had been postponed for some reason. Some were granted deferment to finish their University education, while others were in occupational training. They were a very bright group and in the evenings the conversations were both intellectual and entertaining. I sat and listened enthralled.

Discipline was brutal. Everything had to be 'according to regulations'. We had to look our best for Her Majesty, so we had our hair cut to regulation length; we cleaned our brasses, blancoed our belts and ironed our boots (that's right, ironed). It was how you smoothed out the ripples in your leather toecaps, at the same time soaking in the polish. Toe-caps had to shine like mirrored glass.

Some men from our billet were selected for special tests to see if they were officer material. My limitations were too obvious for me to be considered, but one or two of the others had more than one interview. Despite the diversity in the recruits, one thing united us – a common dislike of our drill-instructors, who were tasked with getting us fit, obedient, and capable of precision drilling. We were taught how to handle an Enfield 0.303 rifle and a light machine gun, and even given, on occasion and under strict supervision, live ammunition to shoot. None of the activities remotely mirrored combat conditions but were simply instruments to condition the men to obey orders without question.

Some days we were taken on route marches. A boy from the valleys, like me, had no trouble – I could march for hours; but some of the overweight city boys found it too much. We passed several, lying exhausted on the ground.

When away from camp, we lived 'under canvas'. On one occasion my duties included cooking part of a meal on a fire that had been kindled in a shallow trench. I took responsibility for dessert, and prepared semolina with jam for a hundred men. It was delicious, without any lumps!!!

A 'HOME POSTING'

At the end of basic training, we reported to SHQ for our postings. I was one of the last three of our 'wing' (about 100 men). My friend Billy was there also, together with one lad who looked too young to be in the service at all. There were three postings left – one was at R.A.F. St Athan, which was in South Wales; one was at R.A.F. Worth Matravers (which I had never heard of – but found out later it was a Radar Unit in Dorset); and one that was overseas at R.A.F. Nicosia in Cyprus. At that time Cyprus was regularly in the news because of outbreaks of violence and episodes of military action. Coming from the Rhondda I thought St. Athan would be a good posting for me; the Radar Unit in Dorset could be acceptable, but I did not want to be posted to Cyprus. It turned out that Billy got the St. Athan posting (I never saw him again); the young lad was sent to Cyprus; and I reported to R.A.F. Worth Matravers to work as a personnel clerk in the station headquarters.

Life at a radar unit on the Dorset coast proved to be very acceptable. My place of duty was in the main office of Station Headquarters. Worth Matravers was a small unit, not more than 100 men. The Commanding Officer was only of Squadron Leader rank, although the Adjutant was a Wing Commander (retired). There were three of us in SHQ. Two 'regulars' (men who had joined up, that is, not conscripted); one of them was a corporal NCO who was in the Air Force for the long haul, then another clerk, an LAC (leading aircraftman), then me, the junior - a plain AC (aircraftman). On my first day of duty I was introduced to the Adjutant, who served part-time. He asked if I could type. I answered in the negative and he immediately ordered me to sign up for a class at the local night school. Charlie, the LAC, was also ordered to attend. Obediently that evening we were sitting at typewriters in a school classroom in Swanage, the only two men among twenty or so young women. Some of the women were predators and two young uniformed men at the centre of the class was a big temptation for them. When the instructor left the room, we were soon surrounded. But life in the service left little time for socialising, so apart from an occasional 'date' nothing changed our routine. The best result of the class was that I soon learned to 'touch-type', an ability that has served me well throughout my life, as I moved from typewriters to word-processors to computers.

I was soon a better typist than Charlie and became indispensable to the Adjutant. In addition, the CO, who was responsible for all accounts on the station, including those of the NAAFI, found my accounting abilities invaluable. Being in favour with C.O. and Adjutant brought with it a small benefit. Apart from some that were important annual occasions, like Armistice Day, I was excused parades.

The camp was situated on the high ground overlooking the sea near the village of Worth Matravers. One Sunday, when we had some free time, Charlie and I went for a walk down to a small beach called Chapman's Pool. We continued our walk around the 'head', a spur that reached out towards the sea, intending to reach the next beach along the coast and then return to the camp from there. It took a little longer than anticipated and when we turned the farthest point we found the sea had come in and we could go no further. Realising the situation was a little fraught we turned to retrace our steps, now going as fast as possible to beat the incoming tide. We reached one spot where the sea was covering the lower rocks, and there was a big gap in the higher ones. Since the water mark was above our heads it was clear we could not wait there for the tide to turn again and there was no possibility of calling for help. No-one else about on that part of the coast and, of course, no mobile phones in those days. The cliff towered above us, impossible to climb because it was a soft kind of slate that broke off in your hand. I assessed the situation quickly. As I looked down into the gap between the two high rocks I noticed that as the tide ebbed out, a small rock, that was about six feet below us, was momentarily exposed. I decided our only course of action was to jump down to the lower rock when it was exposed and jump up then to the other higher rock before the tide rushed in again. It was a little scary since the waters were quite turbulent. Aware that time was against us, at the first opportunity I dropped down to the lower rock. It was smooth, round, wet and covered with a green lichen. My feet had no purchase and I slipped off the side of the rock. I landed with a thud on my chest, totally winded. The tide rushed up the narrow channel once again and lifted me up like a piece of driftwood. Charlie reached out his hand and pulled me in. I was little worse for my experience but still on the wrong side of the abyss. I resolved to try again. I dropped down on to the small rock once more - with the same result. My feet went from under me and I landed with a thump on my chest. However, this time, when the tide came in and picked me up, I scrambled out on the other side. I was, for the moment, safe. I said to Charlie – 'your turn'. He rejected the course of action outright. The two higher rocks tapered and were closest together further towards the sea. Charlie decided he would try and jump at the narrowest point. I thought it was beyond him. I warned him that if he went into the sea at that place I would be unable to help him, but he would not be dissuaded. It must have been the result of an adrenaline surge, but he leaped the gap and just reached the second, high rock. He clung on like a fly on a wall. He too was safe. We managed to negotiate the rest of the journey without incident. Apart from the salt water causing my 'working blue' to smell abominably there were no consequences. But I have always looked back at that incident recognising I might not have survived.

SPORT

In such a small camp, I was soon recruited for the football team. Our team played on Wednesdays against other military teams located in Dorset and Hampshire. We also played in the Dorset cup against civilian teams. The first season I was there, we had an exceptional football team. Even professional footballers were required to do national service, so we had a couple that had played in the lower divisions of the football league. We progressed, even to the semi-finals of the R.A.F. cup for camps with less than 2500 men (we should have been in the competition for camps with less than 500 men, but our C.O. had delusions of grandeur). Sometimes, a local civilian team would be short of players and send to the camp for help. In response I played rugby for Swanage (although not for long – I was much too light, even to play in the backs), and football for Herston Rovers. I scored a goal in my first match for them and thereafter was a regular.

In the second year of my service, the camp team had been substantially weakened. Our professional players had been demobbed and we were struggling for decent replacements. But we carried on as best we could. A popular destination was the army camp at Bovington. With a substantial number of men on base, it was home to several army teams. On one occasion the sergeant in charge of our team received a call. There was a visiting team in Bovington that was looking for a game – would we be interested? The invitation was quickly accepted, and we duly presented ourselves at the army base. It was always a popular destination – they fed you well and the facilities were excellent. However, on this occasion we were in for a surprise. The team we were due to play were preparing for the final of the inter-regimental cup and was drawn from units all over the U.K. It was soon revealed that we were out of our depth. We lost heavily. But there was a silver lining to the match. The opposing centre half was also from the Rhondda and had been an acquaintance of mine in 'civvy street'. The 'banter' between us on the pitch made up for being outclassed.

Summer brought the cricket season. I was a medium paced bowler, whose stock in trade was off-cutters. Not much out of the ordinary there – but I was exceptionally accurate and consequently was a stock bowler who conceded very few runs. In my second year I graduated to be captain of both cricket and soccer teams. I would like to think it was because of my ability but it probably had more to do with the fact that I was in favour with the C.O. and Adjutant and could get time off to prepare for matches, that is, put up the goal nets, or mark out the cricket pitch.

PREPARING FOR LIFE AFTER THE AIR FORCE

Some months before my 'demob' I made plans for my immediate future. In my mind it all seemed straight forward. I would get a job in London and live with my father and Maisie until I got my own place. Regarding employment I was fortunate. I was accepted to work at a bank in the Aldwich area of London. Once that had been confirmed I spoke to my father regarding accommodation. I had assumed I could stay with him and Maisie until I found a place of my own. He refused to consider it. As far as he was concerned it was out of the question. I should have anticipated as much. I decided to return to South Wales, and informed the bank accordingly. They offered me more money to stay – it seemed they were very keen to keep me. It transpired that they wanted me for my sporting prowess more than anything else. There were inter-bank competitions, and since

I had been captain of both the football and cricket teams at camp, they thought I had something special to offer. I declined. I would return to my home valley.

So, in the summer of 1957, when my national service was coming to an end, I was instructed to report to R.A.F. Sopley for discharge. In preparation I put my working blue in the cleaners and wore my best blue to the office. Alas, I had an accident. At that time multiple copies of documents for circulation were produced on a Gestetner duplicating machine by means of a stencil which was 'cut' on a typewriter. If you made a typing mistake it could be amended by using a red correcting fluid (a smelly, gluey kind of product, which looked like nail polish). Accidentally, I tipped a bottle of the sticky correcting fluid over the trousers of my dress uniform. Instead of being pristine air force blue, it was now multi-coloured, like shot silk. I did not want to buy a new uniform – I only had days to go. The C.O. decided to help. Obviously, I couldn't say 'no' to him. He applied various liquids and detergents without success. Even the local dry cleaners admitted defeat. When I reported to R.A.F. Sopley, a camp that was run on disciplined military lines, I was wearing a uniform that should have been donated to a charity shop. Nevertheless, with a succession of ploys where

I stood behind others or held something in front of me, I managed to escape the attention of any officers and succeeded in completing the discharge procedure without incident.

CHAPTER EIGHT

LIFE AFTER NATIONAL SERVICE

LIFE AS A LODGER

Age 20, recently demobbed, rejected by my father, and newly returned to the Rhondda, I needed a place to stay. I decided to ask my father's sister Beryl, for lodgings. She immediately said 'Yes'. They had an empty bedroom and the extra money would help with the household expenses. The house in Wyndham Street, Ton-Pentre, was home to the Jones family, that is, Beryl, Jim her husband, two children Allan and Norman (later to be followed by a third, Philip) and Jim's father. For me, it was a life-line. Beryl was extremely kind, and I was treated very well indeed.

But a lodger in the house changes the dynamics of the home, and there came a day when it looked in everyone's best interests for me to find another place to stay. I was friendly with my cousin Graham and his parents, my mother's sister Valmai and her husband Verdun. They offered me lodgings, which I was glad to accept. I remained there in Herbert Street, Treorchy until marriage.

EMPLOYMENT BECKONED ONCE AGAIN

Normally, national servicemen were entitled to return to their old jobs after the completion of their tour of duty, but I had resigned from the Railways. I did so to escape paying the superannuation contributions for which you remained liable while serving. These were based on the salary you would have earned had you remained in employment – an amount a conscripted airman with a very small pay packet was unable to pay. The contributions could be deferred and then paid when your employment resumed. I disliked the arrangement – it put you into debt for two years contributions when you had been compulsorily seconded to military service. The chief personnel officer was clearly unhappy that I had resigned, but he could not overlook my previous experience as a booking clerk. I was re-employed – but not as a booking clerk! In my opinion, he found me the worse post in the South Wales region - the afternoon shift (from 2 p.m. to 10 p.m.) in the parcel office of Cardiff General station.

My place of work was a little hut in the middle of a very large concrete area. The hut had glass windows on three sides, one of which slid open. Outside that window was a large weighing scale. Inside on one wall were multiple charts holding ready reckoners of parcel prices. On the counter were large volumes of books containing rates for every kind of product that could be sent by rail. I was allocated one porter who would weigh the parcels, call out the weight, what was in the parcel and where it was going. I was required to record these details on the paperwork that came with the parcel, and calculate the cost. The cost varied with the product – metal buttons from one factory, clothes from another, butter from a local dairy, and so on. They were all subject to different rates and initially separated into two groups – those that were sent at company risk and those that were sent at owner's risk. Calculating the cost meant finding the cheapest rate within the recorded parameters (often there were several rates applicable to a parcel). All this took time.

On my first shift, when I arrived there was very little activity. This is not so bad, I thought. But after about an hour the delivery lorries began to return to the depot from all parts. They had been collecting parcels from the local factories and dairies. Suddenly the whole area was filled with mountains of parcels that had to be recorded by the end of shift. The porter was calling out information for items that I had to find on the accompanying documentation, then I had to record the weight and calculate the price. An impossible task in the time available.

By the end of the shift we had recorded all the parcels, but I had only calculated about a quarter of them. But my train was due to leave (the last train up the Rhondda) – and so the paperwork went into the office incomplete. I found out later that it was always thus – no-one was equal to doing all the calculations in the time allotted. It was an unsatisfactory arrangement – there was never a day when you went home satisfied that your work for that day was finished. I decided to apply for other employment.

WORKING FOR THE COAL BOARD

The main employer in the Rhondda in 1957 was still the coal industry although by then it had been nationalised and was now the National Coal Board. I sent in an application for employment and obtained an interview. On my C.V. I mentioned I could type (one of the lasting benefits of national service) – very rare for a male. But in an industry where there were limited opportunities for women, and managers and group managers preferred men as support personnel, it seemed I suited. I was hired as secretary to the Plant and Fuel Efficiency Engineer, and later promoted to be the clerical support for the Group Manager who had four collieries under his supervision, including the Cambrian at the end of the Ely Valley railway line. I enjoyed my time in the Group office, although even in those days there was still the jousting between management and unions.

But an opportunity arose with the creation of a new post – Area Records Officer. The holder of the position was required to unify the office procedures of colliery, group and area offices. Its aim was to ensure that the documentation and information that was needed for management to operate efficiently and make decisions, was based on up-to-date information that was always to hand. I was only 22 years of age and thought I had very little chance of getting the post. Nevertheless, I applied. I did my research, read all the latest literature on the subject and obtained documentation for the most efficient systems available. Then, dressed in a new suit, looking more confident than I felt, I faced interview panels at both area and divisional levels. I got the job! It represented a big step up for me. I was to be the youngest area officer in the N.C.B.

One of the first tasks on my agenda was to ascertain what records were being held. I was amazed to find some buildings were set aside as record repositories containing books, ledgers and documentation dating back to when the collieries were first sunk, some in the 1850's. They included details of wages paid, from the top official, the Agent, down to the lowest labourer. There were accident records, output records and mountains of correspondence. The salary payments for the Agent were kept in a special ledger with a lock on the side. Clearly, they were not for public consumption.

The accident registers provided an insight into the mind-set of those who were injured underground. When the injuries prevented a miner from continuing his employment he was offered a lump sum payment or a pension for the rest of his life. I was amazed that so many accepted the lump sum when the pension promise was far more valuable. On further enquiries I discovered that many would use the money to set themselves up in business, even if it was only a small shop. It meant, they still felt they could earn a living and be productive and maintain a certain level of self-esteem.

Having ascertained the quantity of documents and records that were still held in buildings that had been 'mothballed' as repositories, a decision was needed as to the disposal of the mountains of papers and ledgers. When I contacted the county archivist I was informed that we were required to keep one year in five because of their historical importance. This meant that almost four-fifths could be pulped. My assistant and myself began the sorting. The day came when an articulated lorry from the waste paper company arrived and the disposal of stacks of mighty ledgers, and boxes of correspondence, could begin. The driver arrived at the Group Office in Wattstown - his first point of call. I had arranged for some help and gradually the repository began to empty as the lorry began to fill. Knowing he had one more call to make, the driver began to load the lorry from the front. Ledgers and boxes were piled high behind the driver's cab, and made secure for the journey from the 'Fach' valley to the 'Fawr' valley. Our next pick-up was at the Ocean Buildings in Treorchy. The shortest route was over the mountain that divided the two valleys. It seems the weight of the multitude of hard-cover ledgers took the driver by surprise: the paper waste he usually handled was much lighter. Nevertheless, the lorry made it to the top of Penrhys without incident; but coming down the other side was another story! He discovered that since the weight on the back was not over the wheels, negotiating a road with such an incline (at places it is 23%), caused grave problems. I was sitting next to him in the cab and I have never seen a driver so close to panic. He stood on the brakes while at the same time hauling on the hand-brake. I think he was worried he would end up inside the 'Bracci's' (Italian café) at the foot of the hill. But all ended well – we successfully negotiated the turn at the foot of Penrhys Road and proceeded sedately up 'Big Rhondda'. The archive in Treorchy was over twice as large as the Wattstown one, and by the time we finished the lorry was full to overflowing.

The easier part of Penrhys Road

In parallel with dealing with the past, I had also to deal with the present. I had to improve the efficiency of the area office, the group offices and the colliery offices. Beginning with the area office, a survey of secretarial support to the supporting area officials, such as the planners, surveyors and engineers revealed a massive and inefficient duplication of effort. It urgently needed reform. A few of the top officials, such as the area general manager, were excluded from the exercise - they already had the best support staff. Partly dictated by the divisional office, it was decided to establish a central registry and a secretarial pool. There was an immediate improvement in the supply of information to the decision makers.

CRICKET FOR THE LOCAL TEAM

In the summer of '57, within a day or two of arriving in 'civvy street', and settling into life in lodgings I was asked to call on a local sportsman, Frank Terry, who ran the local cricket team. They were always looking for players, so he arranged a suitable date for a try-out. Soon I was in the team. It was a game that had been arranged against another local side for the bank holiday weekend. Many of the Ton-Pentre team were away for a short break so they were short of players, which gave me an opportunity to play. I had enthusiasm, stamina and a measure of ability. I greatly enjoyed the match, even though we lost. But I became a regular after that. Frank would take me on the back of his Vespa scooter to away matches, and we became close friends. We were an average team and we won some and lost some.

One Saturday Frank had been able to book a match against a Cardiff side that had a good reputation, Cardiff H.S.O.B (Cardiff High School Old Boys). We duly turned up, lost the toss, and was asked to field first. At that time, we had a fast bowler who was like lightening. But the pitch did not suit him – but it suited me very well. I opened the bowling with my medium paced off-cutters and soon had a wicket or two. However, I was told that their best batsman was yet to come to the crease and he would make mincemeat of me. Eventually he came out to bat and you could tell he had style and technical ability. But I had accuracy and a pitch that suited my style of bowling. It was a classic contest and I finally got his wicket. Since I was taking wickets, the captain asked if I could continue. Stamina was never a problem. That afternoon I took all ten wickets. Frank rang the South Wales Echo, and it was reported in the sports pages under the heading, "Brian takes all ten" (they never spelt my name right!).

THE BIBLE, CHAPEL AND ME

It is impossible to speak of the Rhondda without a word or two about the chapels. Wales had seen religious revivals in the past, in the 1850's, 1904 and later in the 1920's. That these awakenings included the Rhondda can be ascertained by looking at the dates on its religious buildings. 'Box chapels' had been built around the time of the revivals. Each carried a Bible name, such as 'Zion' or 'Siloh'. In the past, chapel society had dominated the social life of the valley, but two world wars changed that.

For a few weeks in my early teens, I had attended Sunday School at Moriah chapel in Pentre, but the lessons were in a language I did not speak – Welsh – so I soon left. On entering the R.A.F. we had been given a Gideon New Testament which I glanced at now and again. Sometimes, in the billet, when listening to Radio Luxembourg (this was the station that played the latest hits), we would hear a little of those religious programmes that preceded the pop music offerings – but none of it made sense to me. So, at twenty years of age I had mostly escaped any meaningful contact with religion.

But, at the end of my national service I had reconnected with Maureen and, to impress her, had bought two tickets to an event in the Capital Theatre in Cardiff – a concert by the Glen Miller Band. Confidently I asked her to join me for a night out. To my surprise she refused – as a practising Christian she had been taught not to attend such 'worldly' events. Disappointed, I took my cousin – the seats were first class and the band exceptional – but the girl was absent. However, she said I could join her for a night out at a rally in Pontypridd. It turned out to be an evangelistic meeting conducted by David Shepherd. He was an excellent communicator and a passionate preacher. His message was Biblical, logical and made a great deal of sense to me. By the end of the evening I had decided to embrace the Christian faith. Of course, it would need further serious thought when I was away from the evangelical fervour of a Welsh chapel service, but I was sure that my decision was sound. From that time, I began to examine the teaching of Christ as recorded in the Bible, and was captivated by His wisdom and sympathy for the human condition. In me was born a love for the Scriptures that has never abated.

CHAPTER NINE

MAUREEN AND ME

One of my friends in Grammar School was Peter Davies, who lived in Bodringallt Terrrace, Ystrad. His sister, Pat, together with another Pat (Lane) and another girl, Maureen Harris, formed a close-knit unit. Sometimes it happened we would run across each other at locations like Gelligaled Park. I remember they enjoyed tennis among other pursuits. I dated Pat Davies once or twice, but it was Maureen who ultimately became my girlfriend. We were going steady for some time before national service and even for a while after my call-up, but long-distance relationships often have difficulties not always anticipated, and Maureen reluctantly broke it off.

But our friendship blossomed again in 1957. She was undergoing training as a nurse at the East Glamorgan teaching hospital in Church Village. I was working for the National Coal Board. We tried to see each other as often as possible, but I had no car (nor could I drive, for that matter). There was a train service from Ystrad to Pontypridd and then a bus to get me to the bus stop outside the hospital. A quick walk up the hill and we could spend an evening in each other's company. Returning home was more of a problem. The last bus was around ten in the evening. But we were always reluctant to part. This meant I had to walk, or rather to run the three miles to Treforest railway station to get the last train up the valley.

It was in 1959 that I decided to propose marriage. We had not discussed the idea, but I thought Maureen must have considered it. Nevertheless, I was not confident of her answer. I had to choose the time and place carefully – but love cannot be choreographed, and in the end, I asked her to be my wife while we were walking in the grounds of the hospital. It happened to be outside the morgue! But she said 'Yes' and that meant we were now totally committed to each other. It was going to mean, among other things, for better or worse. Now looking back over more than 55 years of marriage, we can say, it was 'for better'.

I had asked her to marry me and she had said 'yes' but I had no engagement ring to offer to seal the proposed union. It was decided we would take a trip to Cardiff to buy an engagement ring from one of the jewellers there. After a little window shopping, we settled on 'Tom Evans – Jewellers'; a retailer that looked as if they would have something in the very modest price range I could afford. An understanding assistant soon ascertained which tray of rings to place before us, and soon the engagement was sealed. But how to celebrate? I remembered a very pleasant restaurant called 'The Rendezvous' in a side street near 'Morgan's Department Store'. We made our way there – and found it had been refurbished as a Chinese restaurant. Not to worry, we celebrated in oriental style.

PLANNING FOR A WEDDING

At this time, we were both attending Mount Zion Pentecostal Church in Ystrad, and approached the elders with plans to hold the wedding there. Ben Evans would officiate, and the reception could be held in the vestry of Bethel Chapel, which was just across the road. There were many arrangements to be made and many of our fellow-Christians offered to help. One of the major constraints was money. Maureen's parents had no finance set aside for such an event, so I relieved them of that concern and said I would pay for everything. Maureen's mother committed herself to paying for the flowers. One of our friends, Gwyneth, was an excellent baker and she said she would provide the cake, free of charge. Maureen and I booked the caterers, arranged for a registrar to be in attendance, booked the cars, and arranged for a photographer (a friend of my uncle).

But there were other major decisions to be finalised. What about a honeymoon, and most importantly, where would we live? Then there was the choice of best man, and at least one bridesmaid. And still there was an even more important issue – the wedding dress! At least I could safely leave that to Maureen.

Sorting the honeymoon was easy - we booked a week at a hotel in Bournemouth; but establishing a home was much more problematic. We could not afford to buy. We made enquiries regarding council housing on the new estate at the top of Penrhys, where there were still many vacant properties. But I was staggered by the rent they were asking, to which was added the cost of heating that was piped in to all the properties, a combined cost that was well out of our reach, even though we were both earning. I was puzzled as to who were expected to live there. It seemed my scepticism was well founded, for it was finally populated by many who were on benefits and had help to cover the costs. As for Maureen and myself, we settled for renting two rooms in a house on Cemetery Road, Porth. It was just a living room and a bedroom – no kitchen or bathroom. But we would be together, and all difficulties could be overcome. We did one more trip to Cardiff to a furniture shop on Queen Street, and bought, on hire purchase, a bedroom suite, a table with four chairs, and a three-piece suit. None of it was of high quality – it was still only 15 years since the end of the war, and well-made furniture was both rare and expensive, but it suited us very well.

With everything in place, we could proceed with the wedding. Guests were invited, and preparations finalised.

THE MARRIAGE CEREMONY

The day arrived – 8th October 1960. The day had been chosen with care. We had been advised that it would be more tax efficient to get married in October, and there were two dates available in that month that might suit. Either the 8th or the 22nd. I suggested the 22nd. It gave us more time to prepare. Maureen insisted on the 8th. Her birthday was on the 18th and getting married on the 8th meant she would be 21 years of age getting married and not 22. So, we married on the 8th.

Ron Evans was my best man, and Diane, Maureen's sister, was bridesmaid. In addition to Maureen's parents, guests included my mother's sister Valmai, with her husband, Verdun; my father's sister Beryl, and her husband Jim. But there were two notable absentees - my father and Maisie, who were invited but did not attend. It was nearly twenty years later that they offered their apologies and gave us a 'belated wedding present'.

The hymns for the ceremony included 'Love Divine' and 'The King of Love'. Everything went according to plan. I was presented with a Thomson Chain Reference Bible before we finally disappeared behind a curtain to sign the register before two witnesses. We were now Mr. and Mrs. Sheldon. A quick walk across the road to the vestry of Bethel Chapel; a little time posing for photographs; then we were ready to greet our guests.

THE RECEPTION

The meal was quite modest – soup, followed by cold meat and salad with some hot boiled potatoes and a choice of dessert. All the usual traditions were followed – the speeches and the cutting of the cake. After the reception, Maureen went home to change into her 'going-away' outfit, a pale  blue suit, and we were off to Bournemouth to begin the next part of the adventure.